# LIMERICK

**Designed and Produced by**
Alphaset Ltd.
Designers Sean Reynolds and Tony Hartnett

for

**LIMERICK CHAMBER OF COMMERCE**

**Text**
'Limerick Man' by Michael Curtin
Overview Sections by George Lee

**Project Co-ordinator**
David O'Mahony

**Principal Photography by**
Press 22
Liam Burke, Sean Curtin, Brian Gavin,
James Horan and Marie McCallan

**Additional Photography by**
Andrew Bradley (Front Cover Photo)
John Grimes (Back Cover Photo)
Eamon O'Mahony
Dave Gaynor
Arthur Gough
Evan Morrissey
Dermot Hurley
Limerick Leader
Amelia Stein
University of Limerick

**Scanning by**
Keystone Graphics
**Origination and Print by**
Colourbooks

# IMAGES OF A CHANGED CITY

# Acknowledgement

The project under the Chamber of Commerce brought together Limerick Corporation, Shannon Development and University of Limerick represented by Conn Murray, Pat Daly and Evelyn Lee respectively with Maureen Gleeson of the Chamber as project secretary.

It is to these people principally and their institutions separately that most credit is due for the co-ordination, funding and ultimate completion of what it is anticipated is a fresh, professional and vibrant image of Limerick City and environs.

To many other people and specifically the photographers and publishers equal accredition is due in an initiative which it is hoped will stand as a novel benchmark for future expression and development.

# Limerick - what a metamorphosis!

Limerick is a city that has changed beyond recognition in the last twenty years. This has happened quietly in most quarters, as slowly but inexorably the city has transformed itself from sleepy, conservative introspectiveness into a thriving, energetic all-embracing metropolis.

While there is a wealth of excellent material published on the social, historical and cultural aspects of this ancient city, there is little contemporary documentation available depicting the Limerick of today. How have we embraced the twenty-first century? The apprentice or student of the seventies left not only the city but also this island; thousands others followed in the eighties. What is there to show them now that encompasses most aspects of our city's life?

Every significant city should have not only a testament to its history and diversity, but also a portable record of the environment and personality, to be accessible to native and foreigner alike. The idea for this book came from a distillation of the above.

Limerick Chamber of Commerce, Limerick Corporation, Shannon Development and the University of Limerick embraced this project very enthusiastically. Their commitment has made this book a reality and will ensure a further volume within the next five years. There was tremendous difficulty in deciding where to stop: what building site to include, how many works in progress can you sidestep? The work on the riverfront, various centre city developments, the Market area, the University of Limerick and the Medieval Quarter was of such magnitude and importance that this one book would not adequately portray the full extent of the transformation.

Our brief seemed to be simple, we wanted to inform, and present a proud, youthful, dynamic city. Limerick on the move, out of the ashes. The world knows limericks, lace and the lanes. But what about the character, the youthful zeal, the vibrancy of sport, and the depth of education and commerce?

This in an all Limerick production, from concept to fruition. The design, layout, project management, photography, and introduction were all homegrown. It was a delight to see such commitment and professionalism create its own momentum.

We hope you enjoy.


David O'Mahony

THERE is no more a quintessential Limerickman than there is a Dubliner who hasn't read *Ulysses* yet who is supposed to be more Joycean than himself. But imagine that such a Superman of the Shannon once existed and became victim of a Big Bang and is now diffused throughout the city, his gemlike qualities coated in strata of ordinariness.

Consider the boiling pot from which he came: Viking, Dane, Norman, English, Dutch, German, Scottish; the milieu in which the brew was stirred: imperialist and republican godparents; and the assorted ingredients that were added: the pictures, the music hall, the light opera, sport, faith.

How can he be put together again?

Employ the indefatigable exertions of Frankenstein – Igor, more steam – and the indiscrimination of The Three Stooges to throw everyone who is not nailed down into the pot.

The trawl for components is most likely to be rewarded among those in their sixties who still manifest the traditions that shaped them though the inheritance is odds on to have been somewhat stultified by television's global village.

Unlike all the king's horses and all the king's men, having succeeded in putting Limerickman together again, here he is – though he is not the man he was.

Wherever there are two or three gathered together in anybody's name he will grab the first chance he gets to tell them how he once danced with Movita in the old Rink while she still wore one of the black eyes that Jack Doyle gave her backstage in the Savoy. He's told the story so often he believes it himself.

And, this whopper of a kite still in the air, he follows on as the three-thousandth claimant to have broken the nose of Richard Harris on the rugby pitch.

He has free travel now and deservedly so because in the bad old days when times were tougher for some than for others his wife would nudge him on the bus when the conductor approached: Don't let Mrs. O'Brien pay – she has a houseful. Like his wife he

is indoctrinated with a slew of Limerickisms the provenance of which is rooted in the garrison city influence. Such as: when his blood pressure rises and he momentarily forgets that he was young once himself he roars at larky children: go on hop it or I'll give you a fong up the hole – from the thong in the soldier's boot that the Cockneys couldn't pronounce when they were stationed here. Sassoon and Graves served in the old Strand Barracks. There is nothing of the Brits Out mentality infecting Limerickman.

He is not the man he was in many ways and none more so than in the statistic: he used to sing. He used to sing everywhere, that ubiquitous accomplishment explicable by the fact that Limerick is one half pub and the other half church. He has received the best compliment he could dream of – dubbed a great public house singer. Let the other guy have Carnegie Hall. Having put politics, sport and religion to bed a voice would call on him: Limerickman, give us an oul song. And by way of seconding the motion the publican would come in: Quiet please. A bit of order. Limerickman is about to sing. And his audience could depend upon it being an oul song.

Nobody could put the *ngnaw* into *Remembering You* like Limerickman, and for an encore dip into *The Old Refrain* or *Oft In The Stilly Night* or whatever you fancy from *Maritana, The Bohemian Girl, The Lily of Killarney.*

His wife invariably obliged with *I Dreamt I Dwelt In Marble Halls.*

He is very close to his wife now. Since his bypass he has rediscovered the childhood sweetheart whom he had begun to take for granted as someone handy to have around the house to cook and answer the rosary. Now she is again his indispensable companion – along with the stick and the dog – to accompany the walking regime imposed by his doctor.

But they're not asked to sing anymore. Shhh is only heard now in the pub when the Young Turks can't hear the commentary on the seven days a week soccer matches. What about Kilkee where they haven't missed a holiday in fifty years, surely they still sing in Kilkee? No. Panicky new breed publicans hire grey-haired guitarists – that's how entrenched the rot is – bolstered by speakers and microphones to provide sing-along ballads.

He may not be the man he was in the singing stakes but there is the odd sighting. When there is an Electricity Supply Board industrial dispute or a night of the big wind and the candles flicker strategically in the Stygian pub and the customers fidget and scratch their heads trying to remember how they lived before they were brainwashed an atavistic longing is given expression again: Limerickman, give us an oul song.

Though he is an authority on rugby – as is his wife and dog – he will die happy in the knowledge that he has left his children a love of hurling. Where the greatest game in the world is concerned he is riddled with inferiority. He passes on what has been handed down to him: You have to be twice as good as Cork to beat them. But when he talks about rugby he allows his megalomania out for a walk. Any fifteen Limerick players would beat that Irish team. Not quite a delusion of grandeur on his part because as his wife and dog will corroborate: it's true.

He is a much travelled man who has been to Cardiff Arms Park, Murrayfield, Twickenham, Lansdowne Road, Ravenhill, Templehill, Templeville and recently Santa Monica where his youngest son, the software engineer, has been headhunted. Limerickman sits silent upon a deckchair in California staring at the Pacific with a wild surmise unlike that of stout Cortez: what in the name of God am I doing here?. His wife and family knocked all his objections to the visit with the sworn promise that civilisation had reached the Coast at last in the shape of draught Guinness on tap. He could no longer hold out.

So he sits crucified with hospitality as only the openhanded Americans can inflict it: sunshine, cold cans, hot dogs, barbecued steak while he licks his lips homesick for the Limerick rain, a warm pint of Guinness, Donkey Forde's fish and chips and his own bed. He came back from his honeymoon in Salthill, Co. Galway to the rented room where the two eldest were born qualifying for a council house where three more came into the world. All that time he could lay claim to have broken more teeth in Limerick than anyone without ever using his fist while he worked at the manufacture of the world-famous Cleeves' Toffee. He put in extra hours as a night telephonist so that he could at last buy his own home, an abode he kept in better nick than an Englishman would his car on a Sunday

morning. It took a lot of time, a lot of rearing and a lot of work. Yet along comes this shakings of the bag of a youngest son, with hardly a foot outside the graduating gate of Limerick University and he's living it up in a mansion in the sun like a film star.

He thought he'd see one but they're all dead, those he might have recognised. *Boys Town*, there was a picture. They don't make them like that anymore. He shook hands with a film star once, Rock Hudson, outside St. Joseph's Church, when Rock was here to make Captain Lightfoot. Also in Limerick he shook hands with three presidents of the United States and one Pope.

Yet even though he has shaken hands with the Pope he no longer thinks of himself as the paterfamilias in the religious stakes where this youngest hot shot son is concerned. Or any other stakes if he is to be honest. It started early enough with this youngfellow when he was fourteen and the wife asked did you get mass and he answered I was at half-seven at the Fathers. His wife pointed out that there was no mass at half-seven at the Fathers, only Devotions. Well, the young fellow insisted – and it checked out he was telling the truth – the priest was there in all the gear, it seemed like mass to me. But then the boy had shown earlier signs of a liberal education when he had no school on the eighth of December which fell on a Tuesday that year and in answer to his father's probe : what feast day is it, answered with an educated guess : Pancake Night?

How did it happen overnight? Where's it all gone? Gear? Alb, cope, chasuble, surplice, biretta, he'd been taught all that in Senior Infants. Forty years a member of the Arch-Confraternity of the Holy Family in the Redemptorist Church he could sing for you now : F*aith of Our Fathers, Through Jesus' Heart All Burning With Fervent Love Towards Men, Soul of my Saviour, Tantum Ergo, Confraternity Men to The Fight, Sweet Heart of Jesus, Hail Queen of Heave, O Mother I Could Weep For Mirth -* this last maybe appropriate when he accepts that there isn't a hymn among all the young men today.

Boy's Town. The know-alls used to point out that it was a true story, that there was a real Father Flanagan. Hmmmph! All he knew was there was a real Spencer Tracy and that the boys of Boy's Town were as real as the boys of Limerick when Limerickman was a boy and that they stayed out of trouble with the help of authority in the form of parent, teacher, priest and Hollywood. He asked

his son – the oldest, not the youngest: what's the name of Hopalong Cassidy's horse and he had a supplementary clue at the ready (you'll be a topper if you get it) but the boy answered: who's Hopalong Cassidy?

Youngest son was born standing on Limerickman's shoulders and his inheritance was a state of the art university, a state of the art rejuvenated city through which a mighty river flows that is in the process of being reclaimed for swimmers once again. Assuming youngest son will wake up and tear himself away from the Pacific to come home and dive into the Shannon. He will, he will. Limerickman clings to that. Of course he will. Although the night they had the farewell party for Limerickman in Santa Monica, with all the American pals in, and they demanded: Limerickman's youngest son, get out the guitar. And he could sing, why wouldn't he coming from a singing family. But Born in the USA? Even if he did do a damn fine job on it. They can't help it, Limerickman told himself, as the night grew older and the guitar was passed around, they don't know any better. Until the youngest son showed that he was a damn fine boy as well as a damn fine singer: Mam, what about Marble Halls? Limerickman only listened to herself until he was sure she'd grabbed them and then he set about clearing the throat of his soul. He was ready when the youngest son a little shamefacedly half-asked: what was that one you used to sing, Dad? Used. By God did he give it to them. Closed his eyes and imagined himself back home where the humblest messengerboy who'd duck in to the concert hall and hang by his ankles from the rafters would have a better ear than the cognoscenti of London, Paris, Milan. Remembering You of course. He knocked them out. The youngest son who had reddened in anticipation of a sophisticated thumbs down from his American pals blinked a tear back and swallowed with pride. Limerickman, to show he wasn't all old fogey, and to shake them out of his spell, chose the bouncy encore I've Got a Luvely Bunch of Coconuts and then tried to shrug off the California seal of approval: hey, your Pop sure can whack it.

No religion, no old songs, doesn't know the name of one cowboy's horse from another no more than the older brothers, is this youngest son his pride or his despair? Then again didn't Father Spencer Tracy himself say that there was no such thing as a bad boy. And now that he thinks of it when he compares youngest son with anyone else but himself isn't the boy a topper just like Hopalong's

horse. It's just all this change that confuses Limerickman. He can't help missing the old slums, the old lanes, the old heavy hand of authority that gave a certainty to his life in his obedience, the old frugality, the old rotten teeth and consumption and emigration and joblessness, even though he knows it is madness to be so nostalgic simply because the old package was wrapped up in the old songs.

Look on the bright side. Youngest son will come home. He will flash the same open orthodontic smile that he brought with him from Limerick to California and he will stand a little beefier from the celebrated American excess in the cuisine department and look authority straight in the eye with his own authoritative in-built hypocrisy detector and he will have no chip on his shoulder other than the positive awareness – thank god for Dell - that Limerick has its own Silicon Valley. He will stand tall as befits one born on Limerickman's shoulders and he will grow to become Limerickman himself. And some day when he has it all he will notice something is missing as will Everyman experience the niggling lack of proper fulfilment. Limerickman nurtures the dream that the catalyst might appear in the form of a late night showing of Somebody Up There Likes Me. Youngest son would cop on: they don't make them like that anymore. It might give him a taste. What with all those late night movies not to mention the video shops he might begin to think that there was something in what Limerickman used to say after all. Maybe even in that old religion. Come Back Shane and all the homesteaders going to church. Maybe even in the old songs.

Meanwhile, as youngest son shapes up to become the new Superman of the Shannon; present incumbent Limerickman marks time. You'd have to kneel on his chest and pull it out of him with a forceps that he shook hands with John F. Kennedy, Richard Nixon, Bill Clinton and Pope John Paul the Second. Let the other fifty thousand have that celebrity. Let Rick and Elsa have Paris.

He'll always have Movita.

Limerick life

Always a Smile

Reflection

the planned development of boating on the river in the City centre bringing a new vitality, and the completion of a multi million pound main drainage scheme once again improving the amenity value of Limericks natural assets.

Twilight, Sarsfield Bridge

Treaty Stone

New Abbey Weir

Southhill Marching Band

Walking Tour

Street Carnival

On the Move

Peoples Park

Steamboat Quay

Civic Offices

On Top of the World

O'Connell Street

Arthurs Quay Shopping Centre

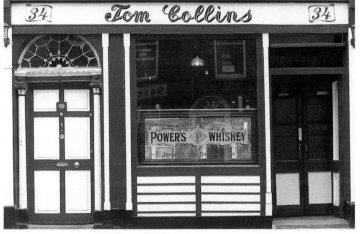

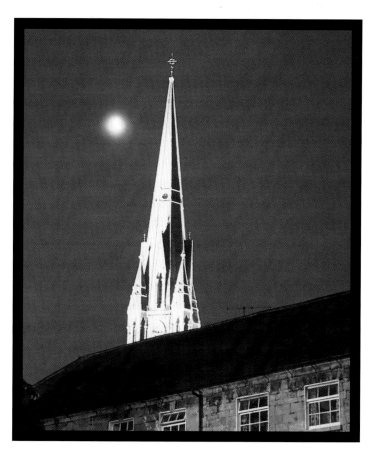

Night Scene

Developing Limerick

## Commercial

As the administrative and regional capital of the Mid West, Limerick is the commercial hub of the area. Servicing a hinterland that includes parts of counties Limerick, Clare and Tipperary, it is regarded as the regional centre for banking, insurance and financial management. With a full range of support services, manufacturing, and ancillary business it is increasingly been seen as a lucrative business area both nationally and internationally. With a very active Chamber of Commerce and numerous business associations, Limerick's competitive edge has never been keener.

Boasting the highest deep water tidal port on the river Shannon Limerick docks provides an important link in the distribution chain for the entire western seaboard. Over the past number of decades Limerick's economic and commercial growth has been allied quite closely to the development of the entire region through the auspices of Shannon Development, who have overseen quite a lot of the job creation and commercial development of the area.

Local News

Shoe Flair

True Love

celtic pzazz

Staff Meeting

Executive Vision

Something Cooking?

The market

Making a deal at the Milk Market

Family Business

Limerick's social life is richly catered for with an abundance of award-winning restaurants where the world's cuisine, from the Orient to the Caribbean, is available. By night many of the old world pubs of Limerick ring to the sound of traditional Irish music - or seisiúns - where young and old join to celebrate a shared musical heritage.

Clubs, pubs and night clubs abound in a city where social interaction is at the heart of its nightlife. New social venues have opened in recent years to cater for the increased demand from a population with more disposable income than ever before.  At night the city comes alive with music and entertainment suited to all ages and tastes, and in the warm Summer continental atmosphere as live music is heard by the diners at tables outside the many cafes, bars and restaurants which line the streets.

Sitting Pretty

Summer Sun

City Pub

After Dark

A Quiet Pint

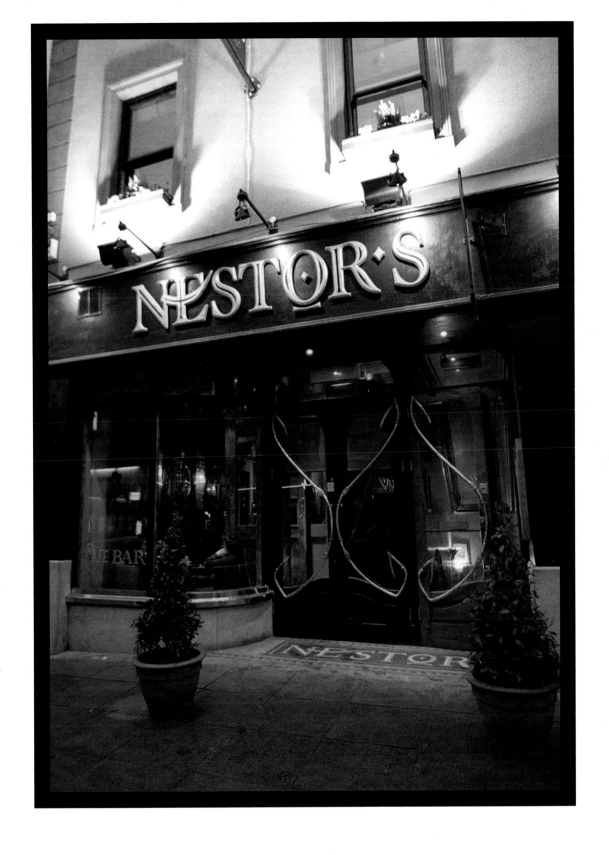

Air Sculpture

Friends

Traditional Music Session

University Club

# Arts & Culture

Limerick has long been seen as a great cultural and artistic centre. Having made many theatrical, musical, and artistic contributions to the world of entertainment and the arts at an amateur and professional level. Playing host to a wide variety of internationally recognised groups and organisations such as the Irish World Music Centre, The Irish Concert Orchestra, Daghda Dance Company, The Island Theatre Group and other professional artistic groups. In addition several amateur theatrical and musical companies coexist utilising the historical Belltable Arts Centre and state of the art University Concert Hall. The Limerick College of Art and Design has an enviable record in producing top class graduates in the field of art and other creative fields. Limericks world famous Civic Week attracts many top international acts in the choral, band and other cultural fields. EV+A the exhibition of visual arts has carved out an enviable international reputation and is now one of the prestigious events of its kind in these islands. Limerick also houses the world renowned Hunt Museum which displays what was once the largest private collection of artifacts in the country and is now in state guardianship. Irish culture too, is well represented in Limerick with a strong tradition of Irish music, song and dance both being taught and performed at all levels from the very young to the Professional

City Art Gallery

Printmaking

A Master at Work

The Hunt Museum

The Concert Hall, University of Limerick

Daghda Dance, University of Limerick

Choir, St. Marys Cathedral

Childrens Choir

Fashion Days

Pig Town, Local Play

The Filming of Angles Ashes, O'Connell Street

The Irish Chamber Orchestra based in University of Limerick

# High Tech

In the past Limerick was associated with many industries, Lace making, Bacon curing, Flour milling amongst others. But inevitable commercial realities meant that these industries were not sustainable in a modern economy. Today Limerick is a high tech nucleus, a desirable place for multi-national and indigenous industry to exist. Founded on a bed of innovation, education, research and resources the mid west has an enviable reputation worldwide in the areas of electronics and E-Commerce. Much of the credit for this "quiet revolution" must rest with all our educational institutions particularly the world renowned University of Limerick and Limerick Institute of Technology whose graduate and post graduate programmes have meant a steady supply of suitably trained personnel to work in these new technologies, and with bodies such as Shannon Development and the IDA whose job creation focus has pointed out Limerick as a suitable location for high tech industry. Limerick's infrastructure too, has developed enabling high tech companies access to international markets worldwide by road, rail and air and ensuring that products are efficiently and expertly handled so that they can reach the customer in good condition. The future for Limerick's high tech business base augurs well. Constant development and promotion along with innovative initiatives and personnel means that Limerick can face the future in the knowledge that the key to the future exists in the present.

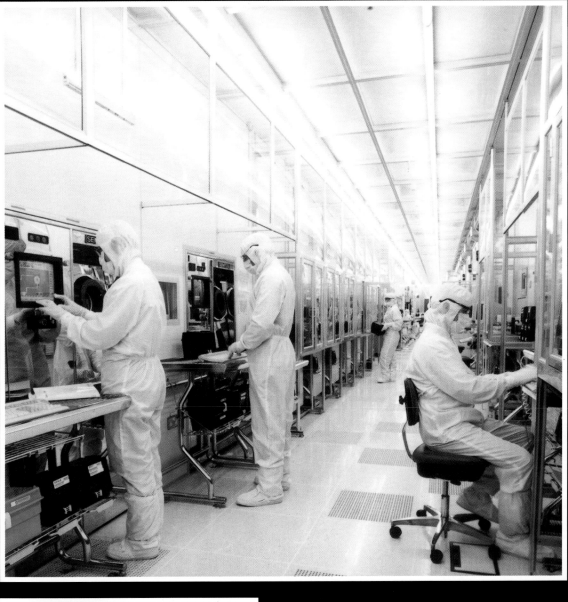

Cleanroom Technology

Raheen Business Park

Factory Floor

On the Assembly Line

Electronic Assembly Line

Quality Control

**Telecommunications Manufacture & Development**

Network Maintenance

ngine Installation

# Sport

For a city of its size Limerick boasts of great sporting achievements. All the mainstream sports are well represented with a wide diversity of other interests also catered for. Six senior rugby sides coexist in Limerick where rugby is played side by side by the "Docker and Doctor". The Limerick Hurling side is always a powerful force in our national game, and traditionally Limerick soccer has had major prominence with many cross channel and international players emanating from the city. Greyhound racing and Horse racing "the Sport of Kings" are also to the fore in the sports mad capital of the Mid West with a fine new racetrack just finished in the suburbs. The city is well represented in the area of athletics and claims four top class golf courses within a six-mile radius of the City centre, including one of the first municipal courses in the country recently developed by Limerick Corporation at Rathbane. The river shannon provides a backdrop to numerous rowing and angling clubs that have all represented the area so well in competitions throughout their history. Tennis and hockey are also played at a senior level in this ancient City that now lays claim to many sports and leisure facilities for those who wish to develop their personal fitness. As we look to the future Limerick is set to gain an even bigger sporting profile with the further development of the National Coaching and Training Centre in the University and the new fifty metre swimming pool currently under construction.

Thomond Park the Heart of Munster Rugby

Hurling Action

School Boy Soccer

Record Breaking Squat

Athletics Track, UL

Ladies Mini Marathon

Golfers

Corporate Games, University of Limerick

On the Chin

St. Michaels Rowing Club

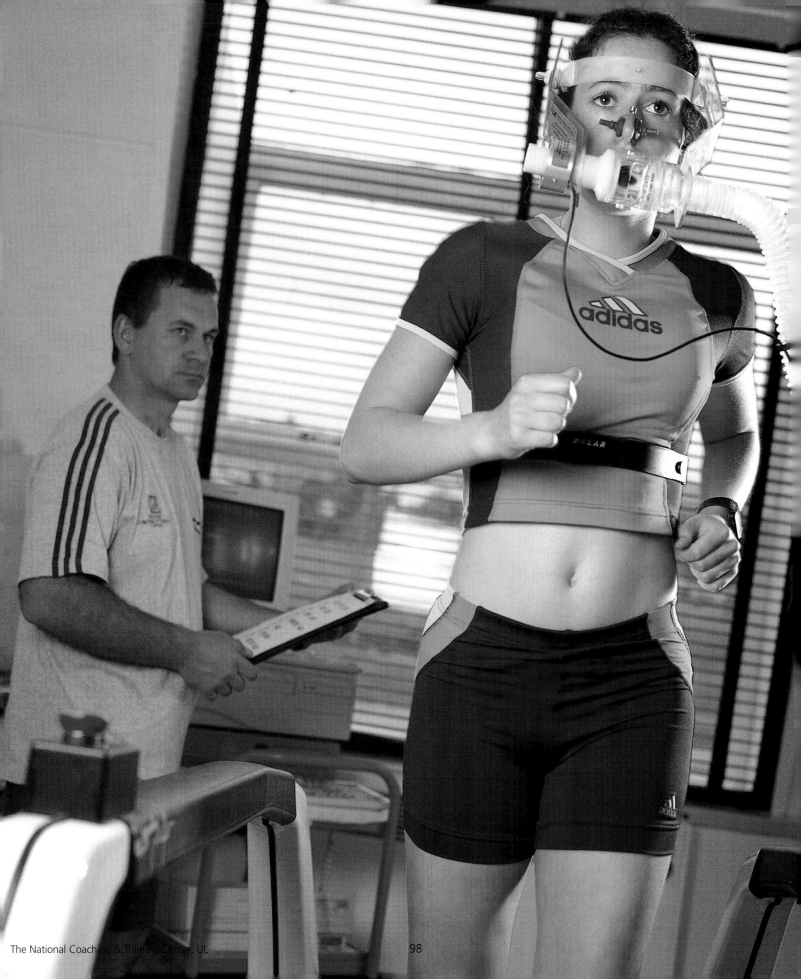

The Hunt, Adare Manor

Limerick Race Course

# Education

Few single factors have influenced the economic and social development of the Limerick area more than education. Limerick has always been to the forefront in the development of innovation in Irish education. From the introduction of free education in the late 1960's, whose announcement was made in Limerick by a Limerick Minister for Education, to the granting of University status to the campus at Plassey in Castletroy, Limerick has always played a key role in shaping the future through educating the young. All levels of education from pre-school to post graduate level are available in Limerick which now has one of the highest student populations in Ireland. The Limerick Institute of Technology and the University of Limerick both have enviable international reputations for producing high calibre graduates in practical, academic, creative, business and engineering disciplines. The primary and secondary educational sector is also well served, with students and parents having a choice of single sex or mixed schooling.

Opening of the Glucksman Library, University of Limerick

Relaxing outside Plassey House

Research & Development, University of Limerick

College Campus, University of Limerick

Ph.D student at work with the Autoclave in the Materials Laboratory, U.L.

Limerick Institute of Technology

Mechanics

Ceramics

Fashion Design, Limerick School of Art & Design

Computer Department at Limerick Institute of Technology

Mary Immaculate College

Art and Design, Mary Immaculate College

Back to School

is the ideal base for exploring the region. Whether its picturesque Adare with its impressive Manor which for generations played host to Lord Dunraven, or Dromoland Castle the ancestral home of Lord Inchiquin, the mid west has some of the most interesting and historic attractions in the country. The Burren, Cliffs of Moher, Aillwee Caves, Bunratty and Knappogue Castles, Craggunowen and numerous seaside resorts and walks are all within easy reach in the area. Apart from all the historic and cultural attractions in the City of Limerick, county Limerick is endowed with historic and remarkable attractions such as Lough Gur, Castle Matrix and Askeaton and Adare Abbey's. Shannon located fourteen miles west of the city is a major facility from which many international airlines operate both scheduled and transit stops. This allows the tourist whether ample opportunity to sample the delights that the region

Bunratty Castle

Adare Manor

Drumoland Castle

Curragchase

Clare Glens

Ballyhoura Country

The Burren

Adare Cottage

Cliff of Moher

Cruising on the Shannon

Coarse Fishing

Ennis Abbey

Bunratty Mediaeval Banquet

Bunratty Folk Park

Moneypoint, ESB Station

Shannon International Airport

# General Information

Limerick is Irelands third largest city with a population of over 125,000 within its conurbation.

## Location

The City is the commercial, financial, educational and cultural capital of one of Ireland's largest economic regions outside Dublin. The region exports approx US$2 billion in international sales, 21% of the total export sales of Ireland's top 100 exporters.  Limerick City Centre on a main circling road bordering the main Limerick/Dublin national primary road. The City is an international destination for conferences and exhibitions. It is served by an international airport, mainline railway station, commercial port and a superb network of roadways.

## Culture

Greater Limerick is the cultural capital of the mid-west region. It is a vibrant city for culture and entertainment; home to the Irish Chamber Orchestra with numerous are galleries, theatres, museums and libraries.  The City has recognised the need to reflect and celebrate the cultural diversity of it's population. It is a 24 hour city with a great variety of pubs, clubs, cafe bars, multi-screen cinema complex, hotels and leisure centres. Its restaurants cater for all palets and tastes and have been widely recognised and acclaimed by international food critics and connoisseurs.

## Economy

Limerick is a focus for business which serves local, regional and international markets. It is a major centre for broadcasting, advertising, press, marketing and communication companies.  Limerick is also a major financial centre. The city has an extensive network of professionals employed in legal, accounting, management consultancy and other professional and technical services.

| | |
|---|---|
| New York | 3 hrs |
| Los Angeles | 6 hrs |
| London | 1 hr |
| Paris | 1.5hrs |
| Berlin | 2 hrs |
| Rome | 2 hrs |
| Brussels | 1.5 hrs |
| Moscow | 3 hrs |

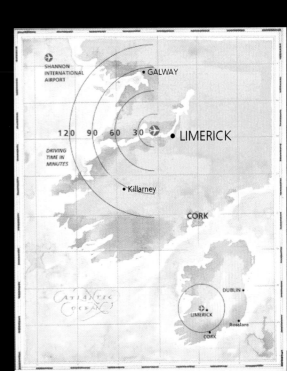